**Some Notable Books in Arabic
by Dr. Assad Ali :**

The Explanation of the Qur'an
In the Lights of the Qur'an
The Explanation of the Sayings of the Prophets
The Pleasure of Fasting Men and Women
Islam as It Was Before
The Heritage and the Future of Faith
The Letter of Finesse
The Book of the Father
The Book of the Mother
The Renewing Energy of Youth
My Way in Sufism

HAPPINESS
WITHOUT
DEATH
Desert Hymns

ASSAD ALI

Translated by
Camille Adams Helminski, Kabir Helminski,
Dr. Ibrahim Al-Shihabi

Including an Interpretation of
Thirty Chapters of the Holy Qur'an
by Kabir Helminski

THRESHOLD BOOKS

Threshold Books is committed to publishing books of spiritual significance
and high literary quality. All Threshold books have sewn bindings and are
printed on acid-free paper.

We will be happy to send you a catalog:
Threshold Books, RD 4, Box 600, Putney, Vermont 05346
(802) 254-8300

10 9 8 7 6 5 4 3 2 1
ISBN 0-939660-39-3

Library of Congress Cataloging-in-Publication Data:

Ali, Assad, Happiness without Death : desert hymns / Assad Ali;
translated by Camille Adams Helminski, Kabir Helminski,
and Ibrahim Al-Shihabi.
"Including a new English version of thirty chapters of the Holy Qur'an."
ISBN 0-939660-39-3
1. Ali, Assad—Translations into English. 2. Islamic poetry.
Arabic—Translations into English. I Helminski, Camille, 1951-, II
Helminski, Kabir, 1947-. III Shihabi, Ibrahim Yakya.
IV Koran. English. Selections. 1991. V. Title
PJ7812.A8A24 1991
892'.716—dc20

To My Dear, My Savior,
The Owner of The Time

Contents

Introduction

The Hymns

Introduction

Camille and Kabir Helminski

IN *Happiness Without Death* Dr. Assad Ali offers a voice from the desert and of the desert. It is a voice of poetry and prayer that appeals to the heart of reality and affirms the heart of humanity. Each of these poems is a lesson in higher education from a loving teacher, the Desert.

A man of universal understanding, Dr. Ali reaffirms the gift of spirit within each human being that yearns for completion. It is our hope that in bringing this translation of his work to the English-speaking world, we will help to foster the growth of the vibrant nexus of spirit among and through us all.

The literature of the Arabs has been shaped by an oral tradition and an intense love of speech. It has been shaped, too, by a history of revelation in language. Language is meant to reveal and to conceal and to reveal again. In Arabic, more than most languages, the word is a lens you look through to the depths and the heights, not a label.

Language has the power to penetrate the subconscious infinity of the psyche and awaken meanings that have lain dormant. Upon reading these poems you may discover new qualities beginning to grow in the garden of your heart.

This first book in English by Dr. Ali, *Happiness Without Death*, is the fifth in a series of twenty four books of hymns known as *In the Lights of the Qur'an*. These books were written during periods of solitude, fasting, and contemplation on the Divine Word, usually during the thirty days of the month of Ramadan. The thirty poems are also the descendants or reflections of the first thirty chapters of the Qur'an as they were chronologically revealed to Muhammed (not the traditional order we find in the Qur'an). The second number, which is in parenthesis, following each poem is the number of the Qur'anic Surah which it corresponds to. Since all current translations of the Qur'an seem, in our opinion, to suffer from various problems of language and attitude, we thought it would be useful to offer our own versions of these thirty Surahs in a language that will be consistent with the translation of Dr. Ali's poems. We undertake the translation of these chapters with respect, sympathy, and the hope that we can bring some light to the beauty and spiritual resonance of the Arabic Qur'an.

In an introduction to *In the Lights of the Qur'an*, Dr. Ali has discussed his method of composition and his aims, and we have freely selected these few lines from that much longer piece:

"Yearning and compassion are the source of these hymns. Their style is clarity and repetition. They are founded on pure love and firm monotheism. Each of these hymns is offered to the sons and daughters of progress who are tactful and call for truth. In these hymns, we find the way to read them and to describe their composition. In their written forms, we also find pictures that divulge their meaning, and help understanding and inspiration.

These hymns have not been written to address any one of the creatures, even though they are exuberant with creatures' concerns, and their true interest is in them and in appealing to God for them. These hymns have been states of appealing to God. They have been written in a method similar to physical training, but as spiritual training in the world of the body and the Word. When the discipline of fasting is practiced, it becomes a training in contemplation and develops an appetite for worship. Then, meditation on God's verses and signs becomes the spiritual struggle (Jihad)...

During the hours of contemplation and fasting, the text of the Qur'an opened my mind to understanding an alphabet of prophets and an alphabet of God's attributes. It drew and is still drawing my attention to the alphabet of cosmic signs in nature and man, and to an awareness of unification and variety...

Meditation on the attributes of God and the texts relating to them, opened my conscience to ways of tasting what I call the Spirit of Languages, or the Spirit of the

Letter. The Most Gracious is an implied speech in my heart...

God, who sent all the prophets, is one, true, exalted in power, and wise... The prophets carried the message as missionaries and as warners according to the levels of understanding of peoples through the epochs of history in which they lived, so that they can perceive the purpose of God and follow the straight path according to that purpose.

My ambition is bigger than my words... bigger than all the languages of the earth...bigger than the paintings of artists... and bigger than the music of the world. Perhaps with effort these words may fill the space of this world, and meet with the source of sense and come back with a sip of the secret of affection... What is given by love, by love is taken. May God respond to the requests of these hymns and grant the world life with love, and for love."

1 (96)

Life Geometry

I, the Desert,
step out of myself
to read in You,
Your most generous Name.

O God, Creator, Instructor,
teach my heart;
     enlighten my way;
that I may come close to You
and read in Your Name
     Your miraculous lines.
This way, I can see
     Humanity in soil and water;
morning and evening I see light.
I can see the colors of Your splendor,
each shade of which is a new Spring.
I read, in your Name,
     life's geometry,
and come to understand
     the secret of fertility;
so I build dams for time,
creating pools for years,
making my life,
     by Your Love,
       long, and worthy of praise.
Every grain of sand becomes,
     by You,
a sensor of thought.
Every palm tree becomes a virgin

waiting for Your Love.
Every particle of being in me
becomes a note
in a melody of praise for You.

O Creator of the major miracle,
You've made Man from "Alak"*;
"Alak" is a bit of nothing,
but Your Will has opened it quite wide,
until in its fineness it has extended
into Being with time and range.

I glorify You in Your Holiness,
You, the only One worthy of praise.
I glorify You in Your Power
                    and Magnitude,
I praise You with the voice
                    of all instruments of music;
extend then by Your Omnipotence,
                    my time and my range;
make me, in Your Universe, a sun
                    bright with Your Love,
guiding people to the best blessing–
                    that of closeness to You.
Teach me the creative miracle
so that I may educate my children by it.
Teach me the art of education
so that I may understand Your miracles,
and by reading them,
                    be absorbed
                    into the deliverance of Your Will.
O God, Creator, Instructor,

*Alak: A word used in the Qur'an which has sometimes been
mistranslated as "clot," but which signifies something very small that
can hook onto something else, and also has the metaphoric meaning
of "relationship."

my letters to You are like waves
                swelling up and out through Your Love.
Send your suns of new inspiration,
and bestow the power to make Your Word heard.
My letters and waves of longing and praise
                are seas of hope,
and You are the Most Generous;
so please, accept my hope and my prayer.

2 (68)

Paradises of Your Gifts

I, the Desert,
Love You my God and pray to You.
I was a weed through which winds whistled;
    You sharpened me,
so, by Your virtue, I've become
    a pen with which You teach.
I was barren and inactive;
You planted life and movement in me,
and made me a destination
to which pilgrims come in search
    of knowledge and wealth,
and You gave me unimaginable gifts.
Please complete Your bestowal
    upon me, my Lord
and teach me how to have
patience with that which You decide,
to be thankful for Your favor,
and to act according to Your Supreme Will.
Teach me how to ripen my fruits
    and distribute them.
The paradises of Your gifts
    are like the Spring and the sun.
Teach me, Lord, how to build
    the new state of water and light.
Teach me architecture,
O Maker of Earth and Heaven.
The miracles of the Universe are lines
    drawn with Your Will's pen.

I'd like to build dams,
    reservoirs,
      bridges, and channels
for the Source of your giving.
I'd like the Source-water
    not to be lost to us
      inside the Ocean;
what's the use of water being
      swallowed by the sea
and never returning to the shore?
I'd like to put to use every drop
    the Source holds;
I'm willing to deliver the spring water
    to the fertile fruit.
O Lord,
what similarity is there between
    the flow of water and life!?
Teach me how to make the best
    use of the minutes of my years;
every heart's throb makes the melody
    of a new life song. . .
teach me how to catch the new music.
Teach me the art of singing
    and how to enjoy love,
so I can keep on singing for You,
    for good.
O Maker of Miracles,
O Lord of Life and Death,
of "Alak" You've created the human being;
with the pen you've drawn
    time and place.
Glory and praise be upon You,
    and accept my prayer.

3 (73)

With My Children

I, the Desert,
wake up and come to You;
before coming, I put on the clothes of Your giving.
O Designer of Night and Day,
Owner of the sun
in Easts and Wests,
to You I submit my endless thanks.
The sun is one of Your gifts;
I clothe myself with it like a bride
on her wedding day.
Teach me how to enlighten my sand
with each ray of the sun;
With your gift of light,
I enwrap myself, and contemplate.
The one whose clothes are made of light
will never go astray in the dark,
but will overcome all illusions,
taking off his first clothes,
blaming neither the misguided
nor those who mislead,
but building the new state of thankfulness;
opening war against himself. . .
chipping the ice from his own door first.
I, the Desert,
have wrapped myself with the outpouring
of Your favour;
my costume's colors are born from its light.
I enfold my children in Your blessing
that they may be pleased

with love's seasons,
and heartily glorify Your Great Name,
constructing, in Your Name,
                    the state of Order,
distributing, in Your Name,
                    the life of Justice,
and singing for Your friendly beauty
the songs of ancient noble love,
which bring into motion the Heavens
                    and all those who dwell in the sky,
filling with ardor all that exists,
                    and those that are bound below.
All of them play with my children
                    the delightful game of joy,
chanting Your Name, O Friendly and Merciful.
Finding direction through You,
                    we've become songs of existence,
songs of Your eternal love.
You're the Lord of eternity
                    and pre-existence;
accept me adorned with Your favour,
O Aim of Hope,
                    accept my prayer.

4 (74)

My Trust in You

I, the Desert,
renew the word and secrecy
to create of both an enlightened gratitude
equalling at least some of Your unequalled favors.
O God, dress me in ritual and robes,
for in ritual, You make my body feel
                    the blessings of secrets;
and in robes You've wrapped ceremonies
                    saturated with Your tenderness.
The ritual relates my soul
                    to Your friendliness,
and the robes declare the lessons
                    of arts expressing Your care.
Your care, O my Lord,
                    is a pasture on whose grass
                    I grow and become strong;
Your pasture's grass is my sustenance
                    bringing forth people
                    renewed by Your seasons
as smiles become sons and daughters.
Your nurturing breeze smiles
                    at my palm trees and horses,
so I beat my drums with enthusiasm
and make sure of my arrival.
My trust in You establishes me
                    in the city of Security;
I turn on the lights brightly in Mecca
                    and every place within me
                    to praise You faithfully;

Al-Hijaz bars off doubts,
Medina civilizes bedouinism and the country,
and Najd upholsters the seats of existence,
so that Your Word shall extend
              to all directions in existence;
by prayer and love
I warn all peoples,
              and thus, every heart is opened.
I teach prayers through peace
              so as to contact You.
I declare, in Your Name, my war
on all that removes my sons and daughters
              from You;
both hunger and fullness mislead,
so, teach us how to be satisfied
              and to avoid greed.
Teach us order and how to keep on the right way
              so that we don't sin.
Teach us justice and fair distribution
              so that we neither need,
                  nor do we wrong others.
I search for a form
              in which I can offer my love
              to my Lord;
You teach me innumerable forms
              of prayers and love,
but I am not satisfied;
mentioning You is my glowing,
              yearning intelligence,
              my burning incense.
Accept me: Your acceptance is
              the peak of my pleasure,
O Lord, accept my prayer.

5 (1)

In Your Happy Desert

I, the Desert
sing, in Your Name, O Opener, O Praiseworthy.
Thus, schools of new knowledge are opened for me
and Universities of new jobs as well;
so I learn from my songs
how to direct my love
                        and prayer to You;
I remove everything, but You,
                        from my heart;
I see Your pure Grace
and the fruit of spiritual
                        aspirations ripen;
I know I'm in summer, for You've given me the fruit
                        of all kinds of blessing,
removing all locks from everything.
My body enjoys the eternity of Grace;
my spirit lives in freedom like the breeze.
You've given me the root
                        of knowledge and work;
Your love is my knowledge,
                        and working for You is my prayer.
I contacted all cities and villages on Earth,
invited all planets and stars in space,
and begged all angels
and those who are close to You in the Heavens
to renew singing and hope
so that the melody be harmonious

and the new world might begin
                 in Your happy Desert.
O Opener, You've opened doors of vision
                 for my eyes.
I picked my bread
                 from the wheat of dreams;
collected my perfume from tulips of hope,
and recognized the relationship
                 between past and future,
when I meditated on the Word of Creation,
                 "Be, and it will be."
Order me, my God
to know whatever You would like me to know,
to do whatever pleases You;
pleasing You is my approach and aim.
Your path is mine and my nation's road.
Accept this prayer
from Your pleading maidservant,
                 the Desert.

6 (111)

The Memory of the First Meeting

I, the Desert,
love You, God, and yearn to meet You.
I praise You until my praise
                    fills Earth and Heaven.
I know You are more Sublime
                    than all poets' eulogies.
I don't come to You with my poems,
                    but with my feelings.
I befriend the meaning
                    so that it orients me towards You;
I befriend the form
                    so that it activates all forms
                        You've written in my heart;
I plead to You in the body's wisdom so as to grow
                    stronger by what You've instilled in it;
I discipline myself   with the soul's wisdom
                    so as to regulate its pollinating winds;
and I recall the prophets' biographies
                    so as to regain their love's joys.
I meditate on love songs,
                    the songs of love singers
                        of all nations.
Release my ships in the sea,
                    my horses on the land,
                        and my vehicles in space;
and shut my eyes and open
                    my palms so as to bring
                        down the memory of the first meeting,

when You made and foreordained
                    that I should exist;
then You put me in this world
                    to carry longings and livelihoods;
and You, the Lord of Religion and the World,
                    elevated Yourself.
I thought of elevating myself to You,
so I spun ropes of the strongest fibers;
I rubbed the cords to make them pregnant with power,
enabling them to give birth
                    to a leap into the heart of space.
I begged them to obey Your inspiration,
so they clung to the mountain of longing.
Please help me to elevate myself
                    and my sons and daughters.
Help us, O Merciful,
to carry Your message for Good
and glorify Your Name from past to future.
O Knower of all secrets,
I'm on the beach waiting,
turning with the waves of night and day,
so as to know a new secret
                    to adorn my meanings;
to catch a new form to color
                    my pictures.
I'm surrounded by meanings and pictures,
for they appeal to You
                    and direct the world towards You;
teach me the best angling method
and accept my prayer.
Your favors aren't known to us;
                    You know that I don't know;
                    please, orient my hope.

You are the designer of fates;
please, satisfy me
with Your kind generosity.
O my hope.

7 (81)

So, to Renew:
Music by Mentioning You

I, the Desert,
approach You extolling and sanctifying;
and ask Your permission to attend the new lessons.
Your schools spread through all of time, everywhere.
The sun is a university
                through which You edify night and day;
You roll up each of them upon the other
                as if it were its own ball.
Night is a ball concealing
                the troubles of day,
and day is a ball embracing
                the secrets of night.
Night and day are teachers
giving lessons of activity and leisure;
by them stars and mountains glow.
I addressed the morning star and she told me
                tidings of the luminous.
I addressed Al-Judi Mount*,
                which told me stories of the past,
and I stopped beasts and birds,
camels and horses.
I asked seas and graves
out of which waves of confession rose;
as if they were one song

* Al-Judi Mount: The mountain where Noah's ark landed.

sung on multitudinous musical instruments.
The spirit of the song goes forth
                    and back to You saturated with
glorification.
Be glorified, O Teacher of all;
how well You've accomplished Your favor!
Teach me and furnish me with more knowledge;
please extend my power's lifetime
so that my knowledge may be completed
                    with Your Love.
Grant me intellectual wit
                    and physical activity;
grant me a long, innovating life:
the lessons of Your schools and universities
                    have no end;
the languages of Your favors
                    are innumerable.
The taste of knowledge attracts me;
the work of taste makes me long for You.
I'll never be satisfied just tasting Your loves;
I'll never be content but in
                    taking Your path;
chanting Your Name all my life.
So please, grant me an eternal life,
so as to renew music and the arts by mentioning You;
grant me the sun's capacity for renewal,
so as to cover the world
                    with the rain of my songs
                    and prayers for You.
Be glorified,
all universes are secure at the feet
                    of Your Magnitude;
accept me and my prayer.

8 (87)

Why Names?

I, the Desert,
renew my selfhood in Your Presence,
O my Lord;
to confess that all my existence
is due to Your favor.
You've granted me existence
and given it a name;
in the course of days I understand
"Why names?";
aren't they for directing Your creatures
to the heights of the heavens?
Haven't You for this reason
ordered Your prophet:
"Glorify the Name of Your God, the Highest"?
O God, how much Your order to direct our faces
up high excites me.
What is high up?
How can we arrive there?
You've taught me that purity is success,
and mentioning Your Name is virtue.
O God, make my appearance
and inner soul virtuous;
and strengthen me to purify my self and remember You
so that I achieve the blessing
of purification,
and gain the links of prayer.
You're my strength and mercy, please,
don't entrust me to anyone else;

I saw birds at my windows
and listened to their chirps;
they offered to carry me on their wings.
Where will they carry me
since they can hardly fly?
I hummed to the bees who offered
                    to carry me on their wings.
What are these beautiful,
                    pretentious creatures?
The range of a bee and a bird
                    isn't the range of an eagle.
In spite of all these offers,
I thought of none but You.
My heart was about to fly to You
when I recognized that all forces
                    are only shadows,
                    and You are the galaxies of force;
so I went to the unexplored hearts of Your forests;
and was obsessed by addressing You.
Addressing You raised me beyond
                    the limits of my size;
I saw new worlds of good,
I saw scenes of the aspects of Your Name,
                    "The Highest,"
but all continents I saw,
and all good I achieved
                    told me that Your Name
                    is beyond any knowledge,
and reaching You is the secret
                    of the galaxies rotation.
Accept me in permanent longing for You,
                    and accept my prayer.

9 (92)

The Arts of Life

I, the Desert,
woke in the arms of night
and wondered, O night,
how do you embrace people and things?
And how much you inundate the children of light!
Night's mouth addressed me in the same way
                as the wind addresses palm trees,
and as the wilderness addresses horses:
"I, the night, charged with sympathy,
put up tents for rest
for those who have tired during the day,
and draw their attention
                to the lamps of the sky,
so that they think of the Creator
                of the world and Highness.
Even day and sun
wish to resort to soul,
so my Creator, the Creator of All orders me
to open myself for them as a mother
                opens her bosom to her infant."
When night overwhelms people in nature,
they enter into the Justice of God's law
and become equal;
Sleep draws a veil and nothing remains
                but the pleasures of depth and dreams.
In the night I, the Desert,
woke up from the invisible drift,
with the neighing of horses in my chest,

and a flow of friends and foes
                running through my hair.
I'm the Desert,
O God, save me from harm;
I resort to You, teach me
                the lessons of pleasing You;
grant me the power of youth
                which expels old age and weakness;
grant me fruits to meet the needs of friends;
teach me so as to teach my sons and daughters
                the arts of life;
teach me to awaken good, and greatness;
to deface blame and all that kills talents;
teach me to share the bread of Your love
                with all,
and to encourage the planet to turn for You.
I look for forms
                that please and glorify You.
Be pleased with me and teach me
                to pray in the way that pleases You.
                        Accept my prayer.

10 (89)

The Birth of Purity

I, the Desert,
glorify Your Name, waiting for the dawn.
God, how much good You hide
               in the conscience of Patience;
I have been patient,
               mentioning Your Name,
and said in my heart:
"My God has more good
               than His creations
                dream of."
I begged You to be pleased with me
               and show some reassurance to me,
and split dawn
               into water and light.
The cheeks of the sky grew red
and I knew that dawn had come.
My sands bowed in the first rays;
then the sky frowned a little
               and smiled with heavy rain.
Known and unknown springs were full.
You've filled me with oil from hot springs;
You've filled me with water from cold springs.
O Lord of heat and cold,
kindle more love for You in my chest.
O God, thank You
for the graces of dawn.
Water has poured like a fountain of youth;
keep it secure from drought,

for fields and gardens of delicious fruit.
Let the light tongues of dawn
reach new places,
and teach my sons and daughters
how to love the earth and planting trees,
how to search in my conscience
for olive orchards,
for forests of cedar and pine.
Teach them, God, how to use the dawn well:
water and light.
Make them hate the allures of immorality;
make them love the dawn light
and the taste of bursting life;
dawn and immorality aren't equal.
Dawn is light that enlightens and purifies,
the birth of morning
from the darkness of night;
and the spring gushing forth is water
that refreshes and purifies, the birth
of purity from the Earth's bosom;
but immorality deviates from truth
and bursts forth with defiance.
Glorifying You my God,
I wait for dawn;
so make my sons and daughters
swim in the pool of light and water
so that we glorify Your Gracious Name
everywhere and all the time.

O God, accept my prayer.

11 (93)

For Your Generous Face

I, the Desert,
when the sun rises, God,
and everything takes to its way,
I burn and glow with the activity of yearning.
I long to invent new languages
                    that suit Mentioning You.
I long to open the secrets of my heart
                    before You who know all that is hidden.
In the presence of the Omniscient
                    and the Most Powerful,
I have the courage
to ask Him to teach me
                    new and useful knowledge,
to guide me through the obstacles of wrong-doers,
and to enable me to raise generations
with education supported by pillars
                    of originality, ingenuity,
                            experimentation and applicability.
O God, make my deeds true
                    before Your Generous Face;
grant me faithfulness in serving others
and make the children of the desert love loyalty
so that they become brothers loving each other.
May no orphan be abandoned nor suppressed by them;
no indigent be in need,
                    no mendicant be repulsed,
but may they advise each other
                    to follow Your guidance,

cooperating to achieve the aim,
not denying the favors of
                    their Friendly Creator,
but always mentioning Your virtues,
in order to do good
                    and prevent evil.
Can the good be other than branches of the root
                    You've already planted?
The highest degree of good
                    is that one wishes good
                         for one's brother,
the same good one wishes for oneself.
That's the pleasure of His lesson;
at night, at dawn,
                    and at forenoon,
teach me how to delight my heart
                    and my children's,
so that we can recognize
                    the secrets of life.
The first step of awareness
                    is to know what the other wants,
and how to achieve truth in life.
Teach us, God, the lessons
                    of knowing nature and men,
to transform nature,
                    and develop ourselves with time.
Grant us sufficiency and security,
                    and accept my prayer.

12 (94)

The Lord of Time and Place

I, the Desert,
recognize Your overwhelming favor,
                    O Great God.
Your astonishing ability to make miracles
                    fills all of life.
You delighted my chest,
so it expanded and filled with pleasure;
all kinds of Guidance and Goodness,
rivers of Knowledge and Perfection,
springs of Faith and Beauty
                    have flowed into me.
You delighted my chest,
so it's filled with Light,
and Hope shines from my heart.
The universe of wretchedness
                    has been revealed to my eyes,
and my soul has opened
                    to horizons of Purity.
By mentioning You, I surpass all difficulties
and inform the planet's inhabitants of Your Will.
Be glorified O Maker of Miracles,
                    in past, present, and future.
From a cell* You have created Humanity.
You opened the door of transformation
by the bestowal of Your overwhelming good will.
Please help me, O Affectionate God,
to make the universe prosperous
                    through Your Knowledge,

*Alak: see note on Page 12

purifying it from evil and sin,
opening its windows wide onto horizons
                    of goodness and blessing.
Teach me how to raise my sons and daughters
on the blessings of delight.
Every evening and morn,
delight their hearts, my God,
so that they ascend to glimmering space
                    within the vehicle of delight,
and inform all nations of Your Name,
and submit to You their trust.
Teach us to fill hours with self-assurance,
                    and with life's joys,
through all the goods and moments we consume.
Every hour contains as much suffering
                    and pleasure
as a sea holds waves and motion.
I glorify You, O God, in all of Time's pools
                    in which we swim,
for You are the Lord of Place and Time.

Accept my prayer.

13 (103)

By the Spirit of Prophecy

I, the Desert,
appeal to You, the Owner of this age
                    and all ages,
and squeeze the memory of history
                    through these eyes,
to extract the oil of profit and pleasure,
that will light the lamps
                    of palaces and places of worship.
My oil lights the road to You and no cyclone
                    can blow its light out.
All clouds are tributaries of the source of rain.
I read a thousand dialogues
                    and hold conversations
                        with ages and winds,
all of which impart their secret juice.
Lord, how delicious is the juice of Your presses!
You've inspired trees
                    to produce Your gifts;
wonderfully delicious is the juice   of faith,
                    patience, and good work.
It refreshes body and soul with the elements of life;
every cell of sand
                    is renewed with force,
and every creature is attracted
                    by the spirit of prophecy.
So delicious is the juice
                    of faithfulness to You
                        throughout the ages,

that it grants physical soundness and intellectual health;
it restores the environment
                              by conscious living;
it opens the soul with truth.
Truth's seasons are the best source of income.
Freedom is the most delicious   fruit of truth.
Who has seen the tree of freedom ripe with fruit?
Who saw it in spring and in summer?
I've drunk the juice of Your love, God,
                              and my soul shone
                                          with the light of knowing You.
Freedom from self took root in me.
I sat in the shade of the tree of freedom,
smelled its fragrance,
and loved my sons, daughters,
                              and all children of life.
I found no reason for hatred or blame,
so I encouraged the talents of all
                              to bloom in the spring,
and to make a new age fragrant with love for You,
                              O Creator of Earth and Heaven.
Accept my prayer
and form me as You like,
                              between earth
                              and sky.
I've accepted Your love to be my life
and enriched all I possess
and my position
                              with mentioning You.
I beg You alone,
to connect me to You
                              in the way that suits You,
and grant me the highest conception of my needs,
                              O Lord of all planets
                                          and talents.

14 (100)

My Whole Character

I am the Desert.
My running horses ridden by lovers
roam across horizons.
My tall palm trees rise high into space
and converse with the air.
What will my horses and palm trees say
                    after moving through space?
The essence of their speech,
                    O My Creator,
is the recognition of Your good will.
I, the Desert,
confess that You know all that I hide
                    and all that I live openly.
You've stored springs of goodness in my chest.
You've intended me to be the destination of pilgrims.
You've made me the aim
                    of directions as well.
Directions run to me within winds and ambition.
People, sometimes, pilgrimage
                    to the home of God;
and sometimes, they pilgrimage
                    to the public treasury;
both are houses of Your favor, O All-Expert.
You know all that is hidden in hearts.
Resurrect those who lie in graves,
and know the character of human beings,
                    and the nature of the universes.

Mold my character and my outer self
                    as You choose,
and teach my daughters and sons
how to strengthen their ties and relations.
Teach them, O God, to activate the joining tissues
                    under every bit of skin,
and teach them all the skills and means they need.

I am the Desert.
O God, help me to build my whole nature
on innovation, courage, adventure,
                    and inspired relationship.
Teach me how to renew my surfaces,
to reforest the wilderness
                    as far as its borders,
to make water gush out from underground,
to purify sea water,
to make the sandy areas green,
to transform the primal
                    environment into a new place;
to develop education on the notes
                    of freedom's music,
to practice religion with love's spirit,
to renew traditions with today's adornments,
to gain habits that improve me,
and to make laws that make me proud,
enabling the social system to be renewed as well.
O God, teach me how to build myself
                    with the spirit of the new,
                        inside and outwardly,
so that I and my descendants
                    keep on thanking You forever.
O You, the Only One,
                    accept my prayer.

15 (108)

Not to Fear Hunger or Death

I, the Desert,
wait on the seashores and river banks,
remembering You day and night.
They say various things about me
and I beg Your forgiveness
                    with every generation.
They only see the outward appearance of sand;
whereas I live the blessing
                    of internal vitality.
Those who are living will know
                    that internal combustion is Your secret;
You've filled my bosom
                    with supernatural, burning forces.
People die and things die,
and I, by Your virtue, store generators of life.
I'm the eternal fortress which You filled
                    with the secret of Earth.
They'll know that life is continuation,
and that death is only a conversion–
                    a creative transition.
Aren't they aware of how tulips smile
                    out of mud's turmoil?!
And how they themselves grow active with what they consume
                    of plants and animals?
You've whispered to me that the secret of life
                    lies in transformation,
and granted me security;
You've taught me not to fear hunger or death.

With Your love as my Kauthar*,
     I am so rich;
You've taught me to long for Your great good.
I yearn toward Your high paradise,
toward its pure rivers.
I bend in sympathy, in the throes of tenderness,
       over my sons and daughters
         and over all human beings.
I, the Desert,
take them to my breast and look at You.
Spirit and heart hail You
      with the best greetings.
The rain of joy pours down from the source
of mentioning You.
Allah is the Highest and the Greatest.
Be glorified; You have given a thousand answers
       to the call.
Your favors given to me, O Lord,
      are costumes that create expression.
How should I express my love to You?!
In my heart, O God,
the incense of longing for You
      is burning;
please, keep me with You forever;
and accept the prayers
of Your poor servant,
      the Desert.

Kauthar: According to Yusuf Ali's commentary on the Qur'an: The heavenly fountain of unbounded grace and knowledge, mercy and goodness, truth and wisdom, spiritual power and insight which quenches the highest spiritual thirst of mankind. It confers overflowing blessings of all kinds.

16 (102)

In the Gardens of Your Mercy

I, the Desert,
recognize Your Mercy toward that which is good.
O my Lord,
You are the Maker of Miracles
upon earth and in the heavens.
Water and soil narrate in thousands of tongues
the story of miracles within universes
and within human beings.
How did a wave rise from the soil
and become a human being?
And how does the wave
return to the soil,
sooner or later, after its play?
In itself it tells
that You are the Capable,
the Truth,
and that Your Miraculous Power
has mercy on the fates of men.
I follow the aspects of Your Merciful Power;
I meditate on Your miracles
smiling and frowning:
O Lord,
Your miracles are in water and sun.
When water and soil marry
and give birth to daughters and sons,
and structures,
and raise in the eye of the sun
the glories of civilization;

when secrets of light
open up in the mouth of the air,
when seasons give abundantly,
I rise on the shores to say:
"O people, race to multiply the good.
Be plentiful in the knowledge
                    and miracles of the Gracious.
Contemplate, meditate on the Mercy of the Capacity
                    that lies within things.
Move about, move about
in the orchards of His Capable Mercy,
and learn from His Pure Qualities
                    the art of proliferation,
and propagate by His Virtue and by thanking Him.
Renew again and again your contemplation
and thank God, the Lord of Creation."
                    O God, I thank You;
increase Your favors for me; accept me
in the gardens of Your Mercy
                    forever,
                    and accept my prayer.

17 (107)

The Lord of Religion and the World

I am the Desert.
Your Name, be glorified, O God.
I glorify Your right religion;
I read Your Mercy in water
                    and in the breeze.
God,
I ask You to dictate to me the lessons of sympathy
                    for the orphan;
and ask Your guidance for the bestowal
                    of Your blessings
to everyone who is hungry,
                    poor, and in need
in the Easts and Wests of the globe,
over all the world and upon all planets.
I ask that You inspire in me
                    permanent attention to obedience
                    and appropriate love for You.
Elevate me, O God, to Your deeply rooted
                    and spring-filled hills;
and prepare for my nation all the benefits
                    of vessels which can be filled
                    and carry good things.
O God, give me the benefit of Nature's Secret;
weave my cells of Your Love's elements;
and give me humanity's great energy
to facilitate an environment of ease
                    for human beings
that we may be unified
                    in the hymn of permanent remembrance.

I am the Desert.
O God,
to You belongs all dignity and permanence;
gifts of prayer and fasting are made for You;
from You come pleasures, joys, and sweetness.
I'm willing that mentioning You shall consciously open
                    all over the Universe.
Give me, God,
physical power,
mental power,
and eloquence
to sing Your praises
                    everywhere,
to spread the umbrellas of Your favor
                    over all times.
                    O God!
How much I love to repeat
                    my recognition of Your favor!
I recognize that You are the Lord of Religion
                    and the World,
please accept my prayer.

18 (109)

I Worship Only You

I, the Desert,
have believed that You are the only God.
Lord, save me from idols and desires.
I have believed in prophecy;
teach me real, passionate love for Your creation
                and Your creatures.
I, the Desert,
have believed in Your law;
raise me to the throne of happiness;
make the river of oblivion flow over the temples
           of the unfaithful;
and empower it so as to wash disbelief
           from their hearts,
and to grow camphor gardens there
                with the fragrance of forgiveness
                and pleasure.
I worship only You,
              and feel the utmost delight
when fountains of addressing You
              gush out from my heart,
O God.
By worshipping You, I rise
              to the level of invention,
and taste the blessings of delight, and knowledge.
I feel that permanent vitality
              is flowing out from me,
and that all of time's humanity
              is gathered, now.

I feel human society glowing with happiness;
a society of invention and excellence
                              in an era of worship.
What delight it is to worship, Lord;
to be completely directed to You, my Creator.
Each grain of my sands,
in a moment of revelation,
wears the cloak of gushing vitality,
as if it were a continent of a new planet
out of which bursts the spring of Fertility
                              and from which irrigation flows.
What a secret there is in that shining source!!
God, at the hour of the coming of Life,
everything changes,
for Your favor
has flowed with Mercy
and Kindness.
I love You and worship You.
O God,
accept my prayer.

19 (105)

While Doors Are Open for All

I am the Desert.
My heart is opened by mentioning You, God;
so I smile and fill
                    my home and road with joy.
Brothers gather and surge with me
and with incentive unity we arrive
                    at the Source of power and happiness.
On a wide meadow round that source,
                    we sit on our cloak,
and appeal to You with details of worship.
Why details, when You are the Knower
                    of all secrets,
and the Teacher of night and day?!
Why details when the intelligent
                    are addressed?!
You are the God and Sender of prophets
                    who teach attention.
I pay attention to the speech of nature
                    and Man.
The University of Nature teaches the lessons
                    of right life.
God, I've never seen water,
                    fanatical about politics,
nor have I seen air
                    belonging to any sect,
nor has light argued with me
                    to affiliate with its nation.

Water, light and air all speak
              one language;
Their clear language is:
              "I'm at the disposal of Humanity."
Why do people push each other
              while doors are open for all?
I don't feel that the Sun's
              doors might be closed to anyone;
but those who shut their doors don't receive.
God, teach me the sublimity
              of receiving and giving;
You are the Knower of the Unseen,
so I don't need to enter into details
              with You.
Teach my nation the blessing
              of being unified with You
so that it will be armed with the faith
              which results in security;
and You will become sure that Your House
is invincible against elephants
              and the owners of elephants.
You've nullified Falsehood
              and taught the technique of defense.
Your birds who threw killing stones
              were only a sign of Your mastery
              of deterrent power.
So teach me and my people how to unite in Your Power
              to be invincible.
You are the All-Mighty, the All-Giving.
Grant us service in Your undefeatable army
and accept my prayer.

20 (113)

Between My Heart and Theirs

I, the Desert,
glorify You, the Lord of the Dawn,
who splits morning from night.
Delight my heart
and cull sustenance
        from the husks of labor.
O God, be tender in caring for me,
        and my skin.
Give it the knowledge to protect and enrich
        that which it contains;
and help my content to know
        how to renew my life in Your Name.
You separate seeds from plants.
You split morning out of the darkness of night.
So draw wisdom and seasons of wit
        out of my life.
Remind me of the names of people and things,
and build bridges of friendship
        between my heart and theirs.
O God, make night the home of my lights,
and don't let it separate me
        from the blessing of hope.
Let Your abundant and tender Good
        be my edifice,
so that I do not fear any wickedness
        or envy,
so that I do not fear need
        or poverty.

Grant me Your Security.
Don't separate my heart from anything
                          that might make it happy
                            with Your Beauty.
Mentioning You is my happiness
                  and worship;
reveal to me ways to truths.
God,
teach me how to formulate
                    the best supplications,
the best songs,
and the most truthful prayers.
Teach me the hymn of eternity,
and enable me to sing it openly
                      for all existence to hear.
By revelation, by oil,
                  by the light of love,
this song lives within every home.
O God,
make me mature,
                      enriched with guiding
                        the inhabited globe
so that Your gifts spread
                      over all the world.
My heart's wish is a total rush
                    to achieve happiness for all,
O Creator of all, have mercy on me
                      when I long for You,
and accept my prayer.

21 (114)

Having the Keys of Liberty

I, the Desert,
repeat my prayer and entreaty.
Teach me silence
.when You want me to be silent;
and teach me how to talk
when You want me to speak.
Your love in my heart,
O Lord of all people,
surpasses all feelings
and expression of feelings.
I'd like my sands, plants, animals, and water
to have tongues
so that they all might make rhythms with me
in the melodies of love and prayer.
Your love is an army that defeats
all wicked whispers.
With You, I find refuge
from all that is evil.
I beg from You the best art of education
for all people's children.
You're the Lord of all people,
the Creator, the Instructor.
You wanted them to be an effect of movement
that unifies with existence,
swinging like a pendulum
over horizons of existence,
across the full range of time.

Atoms vibrate, so sound and descendents flow.
O God, lead all the grains of my sand
                    to Your Satisfaction;
and gather the descendents of sons and daughters
                    among Your elite.
O God, orient my nature and humanity
so that they fill the borders of Your Will
                    with seasons of what You want.
O God, choose for me;
                    don't let me choose.
For yielding to You is my abundant good,
and my safety under Your feet
                    is the climax of comfort.
If Your feet touch my neck,
                    I become progressive,
receiving the keys of liberty.
O Lord of all people and the morning,
raise the Global morning
                    out of the world's darkness,
and make me Your servant soldier
                    in the morning's march
to receive Your orders
                    with submissiveness,
and carry them out
in the same way as Nature carries out
                    the opening of Spring.
Respond to my prayer
                    and to my silence,
O You who responds to prayers;
O You, the All-Hearing,
                    accept me, as You like,
                        and accept my prayer,
                            as You like.

22 (112)

To Be Loyal to You

I, the Desert,
in a moment of reflection,
        have purified my being
           from all that darkens it,
and loved You sincerely,
        O my Lord.
Thus, my hymns have been released
        from depths,
as oil or water gushes forth
        from the dark earth.
My oil bursts up arcing like fish,
        leaping out of my heart's lakes,
inscribing while leaping
        orbits and landing spaces.
Industrialists, capitalists,
        and clever salesmen,
all catch oil fish of inspiration.
So, inspire my oil
        and its exploiters
to be good, not evil,
        for humanity.
O God, I feel my songs runaway from me;
in the same way as released energy moves.
Make them, O Lord, prayers and Love.
I listen to the Eastern and the Western winds
and pick up forgotten tales
        from the biographies of scientists.

O God,
application has forgotten the scientist:
Nobel's struggle
to make dynamite serve human needs;
but this Swede knew the future
                              darkness
that would come from his discovery.
He devised atonement
                    for others' explosive misuse
by asking that the Fruit
                    of this invention
be given to those who further any cause
                    for Peace.
I listen to the Eastern
                    and the Western winds,
and feel the Universal music
                    in my limbs,
being renewed in the depth-filled heart
                    of my sands.
Would the oil extracted wrongly serve?
God, show the impatient ones
                    how to drill well.
Be glorified,
O Eternal, Unique One.
Everything existing appeals to You
to gain from You
                    permanent Life.
So, give me the true existence
                    and teach my children
                        to be loyal to You,
and accept my prayer.

23 (53)

It Is A Deep Cosmic Worship

I am the Desert.
God, my heart kneels,
                worshipping You,
and is transformed through worship
                from stage to stage.
Lord,
You know my heart best,
                for You created it in this form,
and named it "heart,"
                for it accepted
                        the bond and the challenge.
Its commitment is continual labor,
                the work of bringing Your voice
                        to others' ears;
My heart changes as it labors,
connecting with everything
                You have offered to us,
for every sense participates
                in this work:
skin, eye, ear, nose, mouth,
and all invisible senses You've conferred.
My soul renews itself through breathing,
and I join with others
                as spirit with spirit.
My spirit unites with nature's wind
                to carry breezes of renewal to my heart,
where millions of globules,
                red and white, Lord,

rotate within the cycles of my heart,
                    transformed in active worship.
Worship is their sole endeavor.
They bow and kneel for You
                    in every heartbeat.
In this deep cosmic worship
the call to prayer is Your accurate design;
the practice follows Your silent pattern;
its ceremony, the permanent longing to mention You.
Every heart globule
has a ray of contact
with the glimmer of a star.
Every grain of sand
has a thread of conversation
with a gentle breeze.
The heavens and their inhabitants,
the galaxies and those who dwell there,
earth and all the life it bears,
all transmit and receive
                    this contact, this communication;
and all of them repeat
                    the standing clause filled with blessing:
"We worship only You,
                    and ask help from You alone."
So, accept my prayer.

24 (80)

In Your Endless Absoluteness

I am the Desert.
My heart is always hungry, Lord, for Your Love,
and stays up at night with the stars
so that its longings may receive
                        the vision beams of starry eyes.
It meets You in early mornings,
rushing through the roots
                        of plants and trees,
to listen to Your lessons
                        given to leaves, flowers and fruit.
Sometimes my heart forgets the orbits of things,
so it rushes to You without any known orbit,
as a child rushes into the open arms of her father,
and is enveloped, whether weeping or laughing.
She rushes to him,
and wraps her small arms around his neck;
he embraces her kindly and tenderly.
All eloquence lives
                        in this rush, God.
In moments of supreme longing, I am almost free
                        from all of gravity's power
and fly into the space
                        of Your Endless Absoluteness.
Soon though, You awaken me
                        tenderly, with gentle kindness,
and send me back to comfortable relativity,
the limits I labor within
                        as You have instructed me, God,

and I continue to teach my sons and daughters labor's arts.
Activity elevates the active one
        to the heights of knowledge;
until one comes to know
        that Earth is the lowest station,
and mentioning You, the highest,
for it is continual vigilance,
        and eternal renewal.
I stopped at the station of Earth
and saw earthly processions:
I saw the good messengers
        and the chosen prophets;
I saw the ones who smile,
        and those who frown;
I saw, among the people,
        the lazy ones
        and the diligent.
I understood lessons
        from the life of the world,
and looked forward
        to Your Supreme Love.
Accept me,
        and raise my aspiration,
           All-Seeing, All-Hearing One.

25 (97)

The Safe Homeland

I, the Desert,
cherish Your Great Name, God,
mentioning it through the swings
             of forgetfulness and attention,
aware of the greatness of its meaning
             whether I meet someone serious
             or someone who plays.
Be glorified, Designer of Destinies,
the One who empowers my two natives,
             night and day.
I settle into my longing for You,
because pleasing You is my safe homeland.
People talk about a special night:
they say, "God revealed the Holy Qur'an
             during that night of Ramadan."
They say, "On that night one receives
             whatever one requests."
They say, "It's the heavier side of the scale."
The counterweight is a thousand months,
but the Night of Power* weighs more,
             for that night the Qur'an was revealed.
During that night God's angels and spirit
             approach earth's heavens,

*The Night of Power: Originally, this was the night Muhammed
received the first revelation of the Qur'an. Figuratively, it suggests
God's power to dispel darkness and ignorance.

or come all the way down to earth
                    by Your permission, God,
for every matter designed that year.
Interpreters say,
                    "God offers only solutions during that night."
Peace, Lord, is the aspiration of Your creatures
throughout the world.
Messengers and prophets work
                    to inform others;
revolutionaries and reformers
                    work for change.
The night of peace is the aim
that attracts all the universe.
It's the universe's right
                    to long for peace;
and no peace exists
without meeting You,
but people, Lord,
walk on roads that make them sink.
I know You are peace
and there is no peace without meeting You.
Meeting You is the destiny of existence.
Therefore, I aspire to Your Love,
and beg You to grant my descendents
                    this aspiration.
Lord of angels and of spirit,
accept me and my prayer.

26 (91)

With All Generations

I, the Desert,
smell the sweet fragrance
of my Lord in the sunrise,
and so prepare myself to meet the sun's rising.
I wash myself with dew-tears
within the conscience of the night;
comb the palm fronds and horses' manes;
and make clusters of dates glow, Lord.
I wink at the stars in the sky,
run with space children,
and bow before sand dunes and sea waves,
as a mother rocks her sleepless baby.
I smell Your perfume wrapped in the sun's
mantle of silence;
I wrap myself with my silent cloak, preparing to sleep,
but the rotating wheel of dreams
turns me like a swing on the voice of the waves.
Waves neigh like horses,
and generations rise in clusters,
and I will be with all generations always.
God, I wrap myself with my sleeping gown,
but I don't sleep,
because I set up my tent
on the waves of dreams.
I dream of meeting the sun,
for my soul senses Your fragrance in it.
All waves
and gatherings

jump to meet the sun
for the same reason that my soul
                longs for that meeting.
You've given the sun
                the powers of heat and light;
and sent the shine of life
                through its rays.
I don't fear death.
I smell resurrection in the sunrise,
                the perfume of eternity.
The sun sets and is resurrected
                in rising again,
so that we come to know the road to You.
Teach me how to read this eloquent ray.
Teacher of eloquence, teach humanity,
                and accept my prayer.

27 (85)

In the Race of Holy Struggle

I, the Desert,
opened my windows
in every direction,
and inhaled the eloquence of languages from You.
I stare at the sky strewn with constellations,
Your handsome features in planets and stars.
I follow the sun's journey
among the constellations,
delighted with the love burdens
it places in Aries, God,
and enthusiastic for the hot changes in Taurus.
I surpass myself when my soul
arrives at Gemini;
I dive into the depths of secrets
when it flows through Cancer;
I jump into the space of the predominant absolute
when it enters Leo;
and vary ways without saying any word
when it enters Virgo.
When my self weighs ears of grain
in Libra,
I promise my self the jewels
with which You have honored me.
When my self rotates through Scorpio,
I approach my Beloved,
and contemplate the carnelian necklace.
When the sun intensifies in Sagittarius,

I take myself to task, and drive my self forward
          in the race of holy struggle.
When the sun works hard in Capricorn
          to help existence,
I work hard, God, to rejuvenate myself
          and to remain suitable
          for the civilization of renewal.
When the ray-brides hang in Aquarius,
I'll be guided by You
          to the depths of what pleases You.
When the sun sleeps in Pisces,
I give my self the space
          for complete meditation.
I liberate myself from seasons
          caused by constellations,
and discover my freedom in surpassing everything
          on my way to You.
I find myself within Your forgiving and friendly love,
and receive the chance to look at the light
          of Your happy face,
and intend that:
in front of the Glorious Only One,
I may be freed from every need and requirement;
but the grains of my sand rush in asking,
          begging You to keep my descendents
          and nation united,
for their unity frees them
          from what isn't befitting
          a servant of the Only One.
So accept me, God, and accept my prayer.

28 (95)

The Most Generous Teacher

I, the Desert,
have come to You
           burning my oil;
please, give my arid sands
           olive greenness.
Your gifts are unfailing rewards,
for Your benevolence
           is the seed and fruit of life.
Give me gardens of fruitful trees,
a spring of flowering fields,
and the purity of sweet flowing sources.
Teach me how to taste
           the deliciousness of fruit;
how to distribute crops among all countries.
Lord of orchards, honor me,
           You, the Most Honorable,
and teach me how to plant generosity
so that I may produce for the world
           that which cancels need and pain.
God,
I have the courage to ask more favors of You,
for You are the Most Generous Teacher.
Give where You see it is necessary to give
because, O God, You are the All-Knowing Instructor.
I love You and need You.
Every grain of my sands is a continent
           needing Your help.

Therefore, the hopes of every continent
                    pilgrimage to Your house of charity.
My call to You is my security and blessing;
so let me live in Your safe city forever.
Open, in the climate of security,
                    Man's liberty;
renew nature and society;
elevate us by Your love
                    so that we may never fall.
Your love is my figs and olives
                    and all varieties of fruit and art.
I address You
from the minarets of palm trees
during the day,
and at night,
my Lord, and Light of my eyes,
accept a prayer
from Your poor entreating servant, the Desert.

29 (106)

My God, Make Them Beloved By You

I, the Desert,
confess Your favors, God of the House*.
                    I worship only You and shun false gods.
I deprive myself of my ego's desires,
and direct my winds
                    and cyclones to You,
God.
The winds of my climate
                    are forms expressing their longing for You;
make them beloved by You.
You are the Teacher of languages
                    to all directions;
You are the One who brings appropriate gifts
                    to the nations of every continent;
please make my forms gentle
and make them melodies of love and prayer,
as love songs and rituals of prayer
                    are beloved.
I worship only You, God,
                    of the Ancient House,
and push aside all difficulties along the way,
as I cut my roads to You.
I bring up my sons and daughters
                    on Your love;

*House: the Kaaba, the House of God established by Abraham and
renewed by Muhammed.

I go eastward and westward
        in the history of the Quraish**
to enlighten for the world
        all that may save it.
This world has a temperament
        which You wish to prosper
           through uplifting labor,
but inhabitants of this world, O God,
        move inattentively downward.
I move eastward and westward
within the extremes of the people of Quraish
to renew for children and grandchildren
the principles of glory.
In my houses, Divine Inspiration
        was bestowed upon prophets,
and thus Earth and Heavens embraced each other.
From my abundance, sources of livelihood gush out
so that the race for the good prevails.
I travel eastward
within the flourishing of the Quraish,
and travel westward through the fruits
        of its eccentricities
to extract for the Universe
Your love's tranquilizing, reassuring music,
and the strengthening, healing nourishment
        of mentioning You.
I take clear leave of anyone other than You,
        for You are all Sufficiency, all Security,
so accept me and my prayer.

**Quraish: the noble tribe of Arabia, of which the Prophet
Muhammed (peace and blessings be upon him) was a member. The
Quraish held the duty and the privilege of being keepers of the
Kaaba, and the security and fruitful possibilities of custody of Mecca,
the central holy and trading city.

30 (101)

Your Poor Entreating Servant

I, the Desert,
have read the lines of Your secrets,
                and listened to your birds' singing.
So, the eye of my attention
                and the ear of my longing
                                have guided my heart.
Where?!
To praising and glorifying You.
God, that is the most perfect secret.
I faithfully and truly
                praise and glorify You
and You reveal to me
                the goodness of insight.
I see, contemplate, and discern
that everything, by Your favor, can exist.
I almost fly
in the expanse of pleasure,
for You've taught me
                a discerning dedication to You.
Everything, willy-nilly,
                appeals to You;
but I like to appeal to You
                in every line, God,
by all means and aims.
I dive knowing that You
                are the Maker of pearls.
I fly knowing that You
                are the constructor of atmosphere.

I walk knowing that You
                      are the tamer of Earth.
God,
I love You and whoever
                      and whatever loves You.
I've recognized that every
                      creature loves You
                              in a certain way,
so, I thought of loving every creature, too,
                      for each is Your creation.
Sometimes I intend to write a splendid phrase,
but an inner eraser stops
                      the pens of intention.
I think over and over how to express
                      my love for You.
I feel I'm knocking at innumerable doors,
and many new doors are opened.
Every time a door between my heart and You
                      is opened,
Your most radiant light appears brighter,
and increases my yearning
for the sources of Your radiant light.
Lord, how splendid
                      the yearning
                              and love journey
                                    to You is.
Accept me in endless journeying
                      to the doors of Your favor
                      and accept the prayer
of Your poor entreating servant,
                      the Desert.

Arabic Facsimiles

أنا المحدود

أُكَرِّرُ الدُّعاءَ والرجاءَ

عَلَّمَني الصمت

عندما تُريدُني صامتةً،

وعَلَّمَني التحدُّث

عندما تُريدُني مُتحدِّثةً؛

إنَّ حبَّك في قلبي يُبارِكُ الناس

يبوحُ كلَّ احساسي وتعبير

عَنِ الاحساس

وراني أُحِبُّ الألسنةَ لرِّمالي

ومبناي وهيواني ومائي

يُبوِّئُ الجميعُ يُبي

كلماتِ الحبِّ والحَنان؛

حبَّك جيشٌ يهزِمُ أمانة المُشوشون

أعوذُ بِك من كلِّ شرٍّ وشِرِّير

وأسئلُك فتحَ التربيةِ المُثلى

لأبناء الناس؛

أنتَ ربُّ الناس الخالقُ المُبدِع

أردتُهم فِعلَ حركةٍ تتحدُ بالبقاء

بيوسون فآفانُ الوجود

مجال الحركة

وتتذبذب الذات

فيسري العوثُ والذرِّيَّةُ،

يا ربِّ قد ذراتِ ربي

في رضاك؛

وقفذُ ذرِّيَّةَ أبنائي ومبناي

صفوةُ خلقِك

يا ربِّ وقِّه لطبيعتي والثاني

لتُنفأ جهاتٍ تُبينُك

مواسم مانشاءُ

يا ألله اخترني ولا تُخبِّرني

فإنَّ استلامي بين يديك

خبري العميم؛

وإنَّ سلامي تحت قدميك

غايةُ النعيم؛

إذا لامَسَتْ قدماك مُنقى

أصير تقدُّميَّة،

وأستلِكَ مفاتح الحرية

يا ربِّ الناس والفَلق

أعطني القَبعَ الكوني

مِنَ ظُلمةِ العالم،

واجعلني

عبدتِك الجنديَّة

أنا الصحراء

خُلِقَتْ كِياني مِن سوانِحِه

في لحظةِ تفكير ؛

وأخلصتُ لكَ الحبَّ يا مولايَ ؛

فانتفضتُ أنا سيدي مِن الأعماقِ ؛

كما ينفجرُ الزيتُ والماءُ

إنَّ زيتي أسماكٌ تنفِزُ

بين بحيراتِ قلبي ؛

وترسُمُ في تمزُّقاتِها

مطاراتٍ ومداراتٍ ؛

وتعبِطُ أسماكَ الزيتِ

مهابرو العنانَيْنِ ؛

وأصحابُ المالِ

وحُدَّاقُ البائعَةِ ؛

تُقاوِمُ زيتي وتستغلُّه

أنْ يكونَ للإنسانِ خيرًا لا ضيرًا

يا ربِّ أشعرُ

أنَّ أغبيائي تتسلَّكُ بِمنحي ؛

كما تتسلَّكُ الطاقةُ المُحوَّرةُ

فاجعلها يا مولايَ صَلاةً وحثًّا

أنتفضتُ للريح الشرقيةِ والغربيةِ

وأُنيطُ من سيرِ العلماءِ

وكاياتٍ منسيَّةٍ ؛

يا ربِّ

تَسمي التطبيقَ جهدَ

العلامةِ "نوبل" ؛

ليكونَ الدباييتُ لحميلِانك

وتعرفَ ابنَ المتوفيةِ

سوادَ المستقبل في التطبيقِ

فابتدعَ المنارةَ

عن سوءِ استعمالِ الآخرِ المُنفِّرِ ؛

وربَّما أنْ تُبْلِغَ النافعَ لإنسانِه

تُحمِّرُ المُنزَعَ المُتمِّرَ في كلِّ قضيتِه

أنتفضتُ

للريح الشرقيةِ والغربيةِ ؛

وأُهِمِشُ الوسيفى الكونيةَ

في أوحالي ؛

تنبَّدَ في قلبِ رمالي

أئيتامَ استعمالِ الزيتِ المُخرَجِ ؟؟

يا ربّاه

أرِ الخلْقَ لنَشرعَ عثنَ المخرجِ

سبحانك

أيُّها الأحدُ الصمدُ

كلُّ موضوعٍ

يعبدُك

ليسَنّدَ منك ؛

بقاءٌ ووجودًا

فأعطِني الوجودَ الحقَّ

وعلِّمْ بنيَّ الإخلاصَ لك ؛

ونتقبَّلْ دعاء

أنا الصحراء
قرأتُ سطورًا
بين أسرارك ،
وأُصغيك المستمتع
إلى غناء المبارك ،
فذابت قلبي حين انتباهي
وأذن شغوفي؛
إلى أين ؟
إلى حمدك وتمجيدك
ذلك السرّ الأدنى
يا ربّ
أمدّني وأبعدْت
يا غلامي وصدقي،
تكشّفُ لي الستائر
بين حنايا البصائر؛

أبصرْ، وأستعمر، وأستنير،
كلُّ شيءٍ بفضلك تعبير

أكاد أطير
في فضاء السرور
لأنّك علّمتني
النبوّة البصير والبلك ؛
كلُّ شيءٍ تنتجه والبلك
شاء أم أبى ؛
لكنّي أحبّ النبوّة البلك
على كلّ الخطوط؛
بكلّ الوسائل والغابات
يا ربّ
أغوص وأنا أدرك
أنّك تكوّن الدُّرر ،

الطير وأنا أعرف
أنّك تعتّر الجوّ ،
أسيرُ وأنا أرى
أنّك مزقٌ من الأرض،
يا ربّ
أحبّك وأُحبّ من يحبّك
وما يحبّك ؛
وعرفتُ أنّ كلَّ مخلوقٍ يحبّك
بصورةٍ من الصور

فشكرتُ بعظمته كلَّ مخلوق
لأنّه من خلقك ،

أنزوي أحيانًا أن أسمع
عبارةً بديعةً ،
لكنّه بمعناه داخليّة
تمثّلك أقلام المبتة ،
أفكّرُ وأفكّرُ كيف أعبّرُ لك
من حبّي ،
فأشعرُ أني أقرع أبوابا
لا حصرَ لها ،
وتفتحُ لي أبواب
عديدةٌ وجه يدها ،
وكلّما تفتح باب بقلبي البلك ،
بسيرُ نورك الشرق أكمى
فأزداد شوقًا
إلى تشارق نورك
آه يا مولاي ،
ما أروع رحلة
الشوق والحبّ ؛

فأنثني في ارتحال دائم
على أبواب قدرك،
ونغنّي دائمًا
من معبدتنك
لعترة الرئيسة الصحراء،

Al-Qur'an

The First Thirty Chapters Revealed to Muhammed
English·Version by Kabir Helminski, 1991

96
Iqraa, Recite

In the name of Allah, the Beneficent, the Merciful.
Recite, in the name of your Sustainer who created—
created mankind from a cell.
Recite! And your Sustainer is generous—
He Who taught with the Pen,
taught humanity what it did not know.
But humankind goes beyond all bounds
when it thinks itself self-sufficient.
In truth, to their Lord will all return.

These first five verses are undoubtedly the very beginning of the revelation of the Qur'an. Authorities are in agreement that they were revealed in the last third of the month of Ramadan in July or August, 610 A.D. Muhammed was then forty years old and was frequently taking retreats in a cave on Mount Hira near Mecca. One night an angel appeared to him and said, "Read!" Muhammed, being unlettered, responded, "I can't read." Whereupon, in his own words, the angel "seized me and pressed me to himself until all strength went out of me; then he released me and said, `Recite (or Read) in the name of your Sustainer, who has created—created man out of a cell (`Alaq)! Recite—for your Sustainer is generous. . ." And so Muhammed suddenly understood that he was to receive God's message to humanity.

68
Al-Qalam, The Pen

In the name of Allah, the Beneficent, the Merciful.
Nun.
By the pen,
and by what men write,
by the grace of your Lord,
you are not possessed.
Truly, your reward is endless,
and your nature is noble.
Soon you will see, and they will see,
which of you is amiss.
Truly, your Lord knows who has left the Path,
and knows best who is under guidance.
Don't listen to the deniers.
They want you to compromise,
so they may compromise.
Don't listen to that contemptible swearer,
faultfinder, and foul-mouthed liar,
obstructing the good and spreading injustice,
sinful and violent, a bastard besides,
just because he is rich and has many sons.
When he is shown Our signs, he cries:
"Myths of the ancients!"
We shall brand him on the nose!
Truly, We have tested them,
as We tested the people of the Garden,
when they resolved to gather fruits in the morning,
without saying: If God wills. . .
And while they were sleeping it happened
that by morning the fruit seemed picked clean.
At dawn they called each other:
"If you want to gather fruit,
let's go early to the orchard."
And they left talking in low voices:

"Don't let any of the poor see you today."
And they began their day with this selfish intention.
And when they came to it, they thought they were mistaken;
then they realized that they had lost
the fruit of their work.
One of the more just among them said:
"Didn't I say, 'Why not glorify God.'"
They said, "Glory to God, we were wrong."
Then they began blaming each other,
saying, "Maybe God will give us a better garden,
now that we have turned to Him."
Such is the punishment,
but that which is to come is more severe,
if only you knew.

Truly, the mindful will have gardens
in the presence of their Lord.
Should We treat the faithful
as We would treat the sinful?
What is wrong with you
that you would make decisions like this?
Or do you have a Book that tells you
you can have whatever you choose?
Do you have an agreement with Us
until the Day of Reckoning
that you can have it any way you choose?
Ask them: "Which of you can vouch for this?"
Or if they have any (Divine) partners in this,
let them bring their partners forward,
if what they say is true.
On the day that all is revealed,
and they are called to bow in worship,
they shall not be able.
Their eyes will be lowered in shame.
They had been called to bow in worship
when they were free from blame.

So if they deny this discourse, leave them to Me.
We shall lead them step by step to ruin
in ways they cannot perceive.
And yet I will give them a chance;
My plan is elegant.
Do you ask anything from them
that they are burdened with need?
Or do they have knowledge of the Unseen
which they can write down?
So wait patiently for the decision of your Lord,
and don't be like Jonah in the whale
who called out, choked with anger.
If it weren't for the grace of His Lord
he would have been cast up on an empty shore in disgrace.
But his Lord selected him to be among the just.
But the unfaithful, when you remind them,
would like to unsettle you with their eyes, and say,
"Surely he is possessed."
While this is nothing less
than a message to all the worlds.

Six months passed between the first revelation and the second. Muhammed had doubted his own sanity after the first revelation and this chapter confirms his prophetic mission further. It also exalts the nature of revelation in praising the Pen, the archetype of communication through the word. In a sense Muhammed was becoming a Pen himself. The literary quality of the Qur'an was unprecedented in Arabic literature and has remained as the highest standard of expression of the Arabic language.

The contemptible swearer mentioned in line 10 was Walid ibn Mugaira, a ringleader of those who insulted Muhammed and the first Muslims.

Near the end of this chapter I have translated "Kafir" as the "unfaithful," rather than "unbelievers." The unfaithful, or unbelievers, are not, as some claim, people outside the Muslim faith, since the word was used in revelation to Muhammed even before the community and religion of Islam was clearly determined. It means, instead, those who deny the reality of the Unseen, and accept no knowledge or guidance from a revealed Book or tradition.

73
Al-Muzzamil, The Covered One

In the name of Allah, the Beneficent, the Merciful.
You who are covered!
Keep awake at night except for a small part,
one half the night or less,
or add to it as you will,
and recite the Qur'an calmly and distinctly
with your mind attuned to its meaning.
Behold, We shall give you a heavy message,
for truly the hours of the night impress the mind most strongly and
speak with the clearest voice,
whereas by day a long chain of events binds you.
But remember your Lord's name
and devote yourself to Him with utter sincerity.
He is the Sustainer of East and West:
there is no god but Him,
and know that He alone controls your destiny,
and suffer with patience whatever people may say,
and avoid them with a proper avoidance.
And leave to Me those who deny the Truth—
those who enjoy the blessings of life—
bear with them for a while.
For see the heavy chains with Us, and the blazing fire,
the food that chokes them,
the great suffering
on the day when the earth and the mountains shake,
when the mountains shift like sand dunes.
Behold, We have sent to you a messenger
who will tell you the truth,
just as we sent a messenger to Pharoah:
and Pharoah rebelled against the messenger,
whereupon We took him strongly in hand.
How then, if you refuse the truth,
will you protect yourselves on that day

when the hair of children turns gray?
The day the skies will be torn apart, His promise fulfilled?
This is truly a reminder:
let whoever will, then, find a way to their Lord.
Behold, your Lord knows that you keep awake
nearly two-thirds of the night,
or one-half of it, or one-third,
together with some of those who follow you.
And God, Who measures the night and day,
is aware that you would never resent it,
and therefore He turns to you in His grace.
Recite, then, as much of the Qur'an as you easily can.
He knows that sometimes there will be sick people,
and others who will travel in search of God's abundance,
and others who will struggle in God's cause.
Recite, then, as much as you can with ease,
and be in constant prayer, and give in charity,
and lend God a good loan:
for whatever good deed you may offer on your own behalf,
you shall truly find it with God—yes,
a better and richer reward.
And seek God's forgiveness:
see that God is very Forgiving and Merciful.

The title refers to Muhammed's practice of covering himself during his vigils. This chapter also explains the nature of the punishment of those who deny the truth of the Unseen: a loss of freedom signified by the chains.

74
Muddaththir, The Enfolded

In the name of Allah, the Beneficent, the Merciful.
O you who have been enfolded,
arise and give warning,
magnify your Lord,
be purely clothed,
and shun all defilement!
Don't expect, in giving, anything for yourself.
Be patient and constant in your Lord's cause.
And finally, when the horns are sounded,
it will be the Day of Distress,
and far from easy for those without faith.
Leave to Me alone
the one whom I alone created,
the kind of person to whom I gave abundant resources,
and sons at his side,
for whom I made life smooth and easy,
but who is greedy for more!
By no means, for such a person
has stubbornly ignored Our signs!
Soon will I release vast calamities,
for he thought and plotted,
and how he plotted,
yes, how he plotted.
Then he looked around,
and frowned and scowled,
then turned back and was arrogant;
and said, "This is nothing but some magic of old—
this is nothing but the word of some mortal."
Soon will I cast him into the Fire!
And what will make you understand what the Fire is?
It leaves nothing untouched, allows nothing to endure,
darkening and transforming the color of a man!
Overseeing it are nineteen powers!

And We have put angels as guardians over the Fire:
and We have set their number as a test for the Unfaithful,
in order that the people of the Book
may know with certainty,
and the Faithful may increase in Faith,
and that no doubts will be left
for the people of the Book and the Faithful,
and that those whose hearts are diseased
and the unbelievers may say:
"What does Allah mean by this?"
In this way Allah allows to stray
those whom He pleases, and guides whom He pleases,
and none can know the forces of the Lord, except He,
and this is nothing other than a warning to humanity.
Truly, I call to witness the moon,
and the night as it withdraws,
and the dawn as it comes forward,
that Fire is one of the greatest of the signs,
a warning for people—
whoever of you wishes to progress or lag behind.
Every soul will pay for what it does,
except those companions of the right hand
sitting in the gardens of delight, who will ask
those who have done evil:
"What was it that brought you to Hell?"
They will answer, "We did not fulfill our obligations,
and did not feed the poor,
and occupied ourselves with useless things and vain people,
and rejected the Day of Reckoning as a lie,
until the certainty of death had overcome us."
So, no intercession is possible.
Why then do they turn away from the admonition
as if they were frightened donkeys
fleeing a lion?
In fact every one of them wants to receive his own revealed book [like the prophets].

By no means. In fact they do not consider the Hereafter.

Never. Let this be the reminder.

Let whoever can hear remember this.

But they will not remember except as God wills:

He is worth heeding, and He is forgiving.

Often in these early revelations the message is at least threefold: a particular person or occasion is addressed, general spiritual guidance is imparted, and a deeper mystical knowledge is suggested. This and the previous chapter were revealed under conditions of great stress. In the early days of Islam Walid ibn Mugaira and Abu Jahl did everything they could to abuse Muhammed, his message, and those who associated themselves with it. In all times there are people who deny the Unseen and persecute the faithful.

What are the nineteen powers that guard the Fire? Some commentators have suggested that these represent nineteen faculties within the human being which, if used properly, lead to spiritual attainment, and if misused, lead to ruin.

1
Al-Fátiha, The Opening

In the name of Allah, the Beneficent, the Merciful.
All praise to Allah, Lord of all worlds,
the infinitely Beneficent and Merciful,
Master on the day of reckoning.
You alone we worship, You alone we ask for help.
Guide us on the straight path,
the path of those you have blessed,
not the path of those who have brought down your wrath,
nor of those who have gone astray.

This is the quintessential prayer of Islam. In meaning and structure it bears a striking resemblance to the Lord's Prayer. Both contain seven lines, three of which praise the Divine transcendence; a middle line which asks for help (guidance, or daily bread); and a concluding three lines asking for protection in this world.

111
Al-Masad, The Twisted Strands

In the name of Allah, the Beneficent, the Merciful.
Doomed are the hands of the Father of Fire,
and doomed is he!
All his wealth no use at all,
nor anything he has gained.
He will be in the fire!
And his wife, who collects kindling and evil tales,
bound with twisted strands.

Abu Lahab, Father of Fire, is the nickname assigned to Muhammed's unregenerate uncle, 'Abd-al-Uzza. In this chapter both he and his wife take on an archetypal quality as examples. His wife who gathered kindling with twisted strands is the symbol of all those who carry spiteful tales which eventually recoil upon themselves.

81
At-Takvir, The Folding Up

In the name of Allah, the Beneficent, the Merciful.
When the sun is folded up,
when the stars dim and scatter,
when the mountains shimmer and are gone,
when pregnant camels are forgotten
and the wild beasts gather,
when the seas overflow,
when every soul joins with its own kind,
when the infant girls buried alive are questioned—
for what crime were they killed?
When all the records are opened
and the heavens are unveiled,
when hell is let loose,
when the garden is brought near,
each soul shall know what it deserves.

So, I call to witness the planets,
that advance and recede,
and the lessening dark,
and the dawn which breathes away the night,
that this is the word of an honored messenger,
empowered and appointed by the Throne,
to be obeyed and trusted.
Your companion is not possessed;
he has seen Gabriel on the clear horizon;
and he doesn't withhold his knowledge of the Unseen.
This is not the word of some dark force.
What path will you take?

This is just a reminder to the worlds,
to all who would will the right path.
But you shall not will,
unless it is the will of God,
the Sustainer of all worlds.

Muhammed was given visions and signs concerning the deeper nature of Reality. It is against this deeper Reality that mankind's actions will eventually be contrasted and measured, until each soul shall know what it deserves.

87
Al-A'lá, The Highest

In the name of Allah, the Beneficent, the Merciful.
Glorify the name of your Lord, the Highest,
Who creates with order and proportion,
Who ordains laws, and gives guidance,
Who freshens the lush green pasture
then turns it to withered stubble.

We shall teach you to recite
forgetting nothing, unless God wills it.
For He knows what is seen and unseen.
We shall make it easy for you,
so persist in reminding them,
for reminders are needed.
Those who ponder will heed.
But it will be avoided by those unfortunate ones,
who loiter near the brink of a great fire,
existing, but neither alive nor dead.
Those who purify themselves will prosper,
and glorify the name of their Lord in prayer.

See how you prefer this worldly life!
And yet eternity is more essential and enduring,
and this is in the earliest revelations,
the Books of Abraham and Moses.

Man's spiritual attainment proceeds according to an order and proportion created by the Highest Source. This current revelation isthe confirmation of the earlier revelations of Abraham and Moses.

92

Al-Lail, The Night

In the name of Allah, the Beneficent, the Merciful.
By the night that conceals;
by the brightness of the day;
by the creation of male and female.
Surely, your aims are diverse.
For him who gives and is conscious of God,
and affirms the best,
We will ease the way to bliss.
But for him who does not give nor care,
and rejects the good,
We shall ease the way to ruin;
And riches will not help when he falls.
It is up to Us to guide,
and to Us belong the End and the Beginning.
And so I warn you of a blazing fire.
No one shall enter it
but the most unfortunate
who turn their backs on the Truth.
But those who are conscious of God
shall be far from it,
those who purify their souls
giving their wealth,
not as payment for what they received,
but in longing for the Face of their Lord, Most High,
and they will surely be content.

We live in a universe of contrasts. Those who reject goodness will find their way to ruin made easy. Those who choose goodness will find that they receive help in further choices. Our freewill contains an inner lawfulness which inevitably leads to punishment or contentment.

The word "takwa" which has often been translated as "fear of God," is here rendered as "consciousness of God." It suggests an impeccable alertness rather than the self-punishing sense of sin that some religious teachings convey.

89
Al-Fajr, The Dawn

In the name of Allah, the Beneficent, the Merciful.
By the dawn
and the ten nights,
by the even and the odd,
by the night as it passes,
aren't these signs for those who understand?
Haven't you seen how your Lord dealt with the people of 'Ad?
The city of Iram with its high pillars,
the highest ever raised on the land?
And with the people of Thamud
who hollowed vast stone from the valleys?
And Pharoah with his many tent-poles?
All of these who went beyond all limits
increasing misery on the earth?
Your Lord brought down
many sufferings on them.
Your Lord is Aware.
And mankind,
when tested by His generosity,
and given a life of ease, says:
"My Sustainer has honored me."
And when tested by scarcity says:
"My Sustainer has disgraced me."
In fact you fail to provide for the orphans,
you forget to remind one another to feed the poor,
you greedily consume the inheritance of others,
and you love wealth with all your heart.
When the earth is reduced to dust,
and your Lord comes
with His angels, rank upon rank,
and Hell is brought near,
on that day mankind will remember,
but what good will it be then?

They will say,
"I wish I had done more good with my life."
No one can punish as He will punish on that day.
And no one can welcome as He will welcome.
(He will say:)
"O tranquil soul,
return to your Lord, pleased and pleasing to Him.
Enter with My servants,
enter My garden."

This chapter addresses the vanity of selfish human undertakings that increase misery on the earth. Former societies have perished from their own arrogance. But those of "tranquil soul," who live this life as it should be lived, will receive an invitation from their Lord to enter His garden.

93
Ad-Dhuhá, Dawn

In the name of Allah, the Beneficent, the Merciful.
By the dawn
and the stillness of the night!
Your Lord has not forgotten you,
nor is He displeased with you,
and the End shall be better for you than the Beginning.
Your Lord shall give generously, and you shall be content.
Didn't He find you an orphan and shelter you?
Didn't He find you lost and guide you?
Didn't He find you in need and satisfy your need?
As for the orphan, do not oppress him.
As for the beggar, do not scold him.
As for your Lord's blessing, declare it.

Muhammed had been a poor orphan under the protection of his extended family. There is a child in all of us that needs the comforting love and support of the Universe. Although darkness may come, the dawn will arrive.

94
Al-Inshiráh, Expansion

In the name of Allah, the Beneficent, the Merciful.
Have we not opened your heart
and removed its heaviness,
which had weighed down your back?
Have we not increased your renown?
After every difficulty comes ease.
Surely, after every difficulty comes ease.
So in the time you are free,
continue to strive,
and turn your attention to your Lord.

It is narrated by some companions of the Prophet that one day the Angel Gabriel came to Muhammed, physically opened his heart, and removed its impurities.

103
Al-'Asr, Time

In the name of Allah, the Beneficent, the Merciful.
Time is witness
that, surely, mankind suffers loss,
except for those of faith,
who do good
and become a model of truthful living,
and together practice patience and constancy.

This chapter reminds us that all human beings are in loss except those whose lives have become modelsof truthful living for others.

100
Al-'Adiyát, Running Horses

In the name of Allah, the Beneficent, the Merciful.
By those who gallop panting,
whose hooves strike sparks
in a charge at dawn,
raising a cloud of dust,
penetrating deep into the enemy,

truly man is ungrateful to his Lord,
as his actions bear witness,
for he is violent in his greed.

Doesn't he know that when the graves are opened,
and the lies of human hearts are revealed,
on that day it will be clear what their Lord knew all along?

The word used to represent charging horses that raise a cloud of dust
is also the name for a kind of sandstorm in which people lose all bearings.
So it is when we are violent in our greed.

108
Al-Kauthar, Abundance

In the name of Allah, the Beneficent, the Merciful.
Truly, We have given you abundance.
So turn to your Lord in prayer and sacrifice.
It is those who oppose you who are in loss.

"Kauthar," which means "to exceed in number, to increase," is also
a spring in Paradise overflowing with the waters of God's love. One of the
insults hurled at Muhammed in the early days was that he had no offspring.
This chapter promises him abundance, and in fact his descendants have
been prolific.

102
At-Takáthur, Competition

In the name of Allah, the Beneficent, the Merciful.
Competition distracts you
all the way to the grave,
but soon you will know.
If you knew with the knowledge of certainty,
you would see Hell;
you would see with the eyes of certainty;
and you would be asked to explain your desires.

This chapter is a clear reminder to all who become distracted by competition for the things of this world.

107
Al-Má'ún, Neighborly Kindness

In the name of Allah, the Beneficent, the Merciful.
Do you see the one who denies the reckoning?
Who shuns the orphan
and forgets the hungry?
Who worships mindlessly
and only to be seen,
and fails in neighborly kindness?

In the last line, the word "má'ún" represents the kind of container which might be used to bring food to a neighbor, and so it is metaphorically understood to represent all forms of neighborly kindness.

109
Al-Káfirún, The Unbelievers

In the name of Allah, the Beneficent, the Merciful.
Say: "O you who turn away,
I do not worship what you worship,
nor do you worship what I worship.
And I will not worship what you worship,
nor will you worship what I worship.
Your way is yours,
and my way is mine."

At the time this chapter was revealed the idolators of Mecca had proposed a compromise to Muhammed. They would alternately worship Allah for one year, and the following years the Muslims would worship the traditional idols.

105
Al-Fíl, The Elephants

In the name of Allah, the Beneficent, the Merciful.
Have you not seen how your Lord
dealt with the people of the elephants?
Didn't he cause their plans to fail,
sending flocks of birds against them,
showering them with stones,
leaving behind a field laid waste?

This chapter refers to an event that happened around the time of Muhammed's birth. The Emperor of Abyssinia had created a center for pilgrimage that he hoped would rival the Holy House of Abraham, the Kaaba. When his creation did not attract nearly the pilgrims he had hoped for, he sent an army of elephants to destroy the Kaaba. Though no defense was made against their overwhelming force, a shower of stones dropped by birds wounded the approaching army.

113
Al-Fálaq, The Dawn

In the name of Allah, the Beneficent, the Merciful.
Say: I seek refuge with the Lord of the Dawn,
from anything harmful in Creation,
from the evil of darkness as it spreads,
from the evil of knotted spells,
from the evil of the envier when he envies.

The word for dawn means to "split, or tear asunder." This chapter recommends taking refuge with the One who cleaves the light out of the darkness, Who unfolded the universe in the first second of creation. This chapter is commonly recited as a protection from the evils described herein.

114
An-Nás, Mankind

In the name of Allah, the Beneficent, the Merciful.
Say: I take refuge in the Lord of mankind,
the Master of mankind,
the God of mankind,
from the evil of the secret tempter
who whispers in the hearts of men,
of the jinns and men.

This is also one of the most recited prayers, alerting us to the whispers of the secret tempter and recommending God as our only refuge.

The jinns (or genie) signify an invisible and parallel creation, made of fire not of earth, who have capacities for good and evil, just as people do.

112
Ikhlás, Purity

In the name of Allah, the Beneficent, the Merciful.
Say: He is Allah, the One.
He is Allah, the Eternal,
Who was never born, nor ever gave birth.
The One beyond compare.

This is the third in a triad of important prayers of refuge, (including 113 and 114) likely to be known and recited by any Muslim. It expresses the Self-Sufficiency of God and makes reference to the notion that God could have a "Son." Islam views Jesus as "the Spirit of God" but not as identical with God, and not as the unique Son of God, since God is unique and absolute.

53
An-Najm, The Star

In the name of Allah, the Beneficent, the Merciful.
By the constellation that sets,
your Companion is neither confused nor misled,
nor does he speak from his own authority.
It is nothing less than an inspiration
given to him by the Supreme Intellect,
the Lord of wisdom, Who uplifted him
to the highest stage, and he approached
to within a distance of two bow-lengths or nearer,
where He revealed what He revealed.
His heart did not distort what he perceived.
Will you dispute what he received?
He had had a vision before
by the Lote tree no one can go beyond,
near the Garden of Presence
when the Lote tree was wrapped in mystery,
and his vision did not waver or falter.

Indeed, he saw the greatest signs of his Lord.
Have you considered Lat and 'Uzza,
and the third goddess, Manat?
Are there sons for you and daughters for Him?
That would be unfair!
These are only names which you and your fathers invented.
God gave no authority for these.
They follow their fantasies and vain desires,
even though guidance had come from their Lord!
Will man ever get what he wants?
The End and the Beginning belong to God.

As many angels as there are in heaven
will be of no avail without God's permission,
for what He wishes and what He approves.
Those who have no faith in the afterlife
give the angels female names.
Yet they know nothing, and follow fantasies,
and fantasies cannot replace the truth.
And so turn away from those who turn away from Remembrance
and desire nothing but the life of this world.
This is the limit of what they know.
Surely, your Lord alone knows best
who has left the path and who has been guided.
To God belongs all of heaven and earth,
that he may give evil for evil deeds,
and good for good.
As for those who avoid the greater sins and shameful acts,
whose faults are small,
your Lord's forgiveness is ample.
He Who creates you out of this earth,
Who brings you out of your mother's womb
knows you very well.
So do not justify yourselves,
for He knows best who shudders at evil.

Have you seen him who turns his back,
who gives a little and thenwith a hard heart?
Has he knowledge of the Unseen?
No, doesn't he know what is in the books of Moses,
and of Abraham who fulfilled his trust?
Namely, that no one bears the burden of another,
that a man has nothing but what he works for,
and that his work will come to light,
and his reward will be complete;
that to your Lord you will return;
that it is He who gives laughter and tears;
that it is He who gives death and life;
that He created pairs, male and female,
from the gift of semen;
that it is for Him to re-create;
that it is He who gives wealth and contentment;
that He is the Lord of Sirius;
and that it is He
who destroyed the ancient people of 'Ad,
and did not spare the people of Thamud,
and before them the tribe of Noah,
given to excess and perversity.
It was He who overthrew their cities,
now buried in ruins.
Which of your Lord's powers will you deny?
He who warns you now
is like the ancients who gave warning.
The reckoning is near.
Only God can tell.
Are you surprised at this?
And do you keep laughing, without tears,
wasting time in frivolous pursuits?
Bow down instead and worship God.

This chapter refers to the Prophet's heavenly Ascension, or Miraj, when he was brought physically to the limit of man's closeness to God. The term "two bow-lengths" (Qaba Qavsain) has the mystical meaning of being the intimate circle of those who have attained union with God. Muhammed was brought to the reality of God. This is contrasted with the conjectures of those who follow their own fantasies in relation to spiritual truth, finally turning away from God and seeking only the attractions of the material world.

The Arabs unfortunately considered female children less valuable than males, so much so that they even allowed the killing of female infants, until Islam forbade it. Here they are chided for assigning daughters to God by naming their idols with female names, while considering male children more valuable for themselves.

80
'Abasa, He Frowned

In the name of Allah, the Beneficent, the Merciful.
The Prophet frowned and turned away,
because a blind man interrupted him.
Don't you realize he might change,
or be reminded, and the reminder help him?
Yet the one who thinks he has no need,
to him you pay attention,
though it is not your fault
if he doesn't change.
As for him who comes to you yearning
and with awe in his heart,
him you disregard.
Certainly this is a Reminder,
for anyone who will remember,
on pages of honor,
pure and sacred,
from the hands
of just and holy scribes.
What a shame!
Why is Mankind so oblivious?
From what did God make him?
From a seed He created and then proportioned him;

and then made his passage smooth;
and then led him to death and the grave.
to be raised again when it is His will.
In no way has he fulfilled what God offered.

Let man reflect on his food,
for which Our rain pours down;
then We open crevices in the soil
and raise up grain,
grapes and herbs,
olives and dates;
and sheltered gardens,
orchard fruit and pasture,
for you and your animals.

But when the deafening sound arrives,
the day when a man will run from his own brother,
mother and father,
wife and children;
the day when no one
will be concerned with anyone else.
Some faces will be radiant,
laughing and full of joy.
Some faces will be dusty,
in the shadow of darkness,
the faces of those without faith,
the followers of evil.

One day the Prophet was sitting with some leaders of the tribe of Quraish who were hostile to Islam but whom he hoped to influence. There was a blind man who sometimes came to Muhammed with the request, "Give me some of what God has given you." On this occasion, however, the Prophet was annoyed at being interrupted and "he frowned." This chapter was given after he returned to his room and was overcome by a spiritual awareness. It is one of the clearest demonstrations in the Qur'an that Muhammed was not perfect and could be reprimanded by God.

97
Al-Qadr, The Night of Power

In the name of Allah, the Beneficent, the Merciful.
Truly, We have revealed this Message
on the Night of Power.
What will explain to you this Night of Power?
The Night of Power is better than a thousand months.
By God's order His angels and grace come down,
bringing solutions to many problems.
It is peace
until the dawning of the day!

The Qur'an's first chapter, "Iqra," was first revealed on the night
referred to in this chapter. "Qadr" can mean "power, destiny, or decree."

91
As-Shams, the Sun

In the name of Allah, the Beneficent, the Merciful.
By the sun and its radiance;
by the moon which reflects it;
by the day that reveals its power;
by the night that covers it;

by the sky and how it is structured;
by the earth and the way it is laid out;
by the soul and its harmony,
and the gift of knowing right from wrong;
surely, he who purifies the soul is fortunate,
and ruined is he who corrupts it.

With arrogance the people of Thamud denied the Truth
and sent forth one of its worst men.
A messenger of God told them:
"This is God's camel. Let her drink."
But they rejected him and mistreated her,
and God obliterated them for this,
all of them, with no fear of the consequences.

The first part is a lyric passage calling our attention to the miracles of creation and the miracle of the soul which it is a human duty to keep pure.

The second part unsentimentally describes the consequences for a people who transgressed. From a dualistic point of view, in which God is seen as a separate punishing agency, the destruction of Thamud may appear unmerciful and unjust. From the point of view of unity, we ourselves create the conditions for either abundant beneficence or awesome destruction. As a final test, a messenger, Salih, or Methuselah, was mercifully sent to remind these people of the lawful consequences of their transgressions against the sacredness of nature, represented by the she-camel.

85
Al-Burúj, Constellations

In the name of Allah, the Beneficent, the Merciful.
By the sky and the signs of the zodiac,
by the promised day,
by the witness and what is witnessed,
misfortune for the men who designed the trench
and filled it with fire
and watched as the faithful were consumed.
They did this only because these people were
faithful to God, the All-Powerful, the Praiseworthy.
whose kingdom spreads over heaven and earth,
who is a witness to all things.
Surely, those who persecute the faithful, men and women,
without repentance,
will have Hell and burning.
Surely, those who live honorably,
will have gardens through which rivers flow.
This is the greatest success.
Truly, your Lord has a tight hold.
He is the One who originates and recreates.
He is forgiving and He is loving;
Lord of the Throne,
who realizes all that He intends.
Have you heard the story of Pharoah
and the people of Thamud?
Yet the faithless continue in denial.
But God surrounds them.
This is the exalted Reading
preserved on a guarded tablet!

This is another lyrical chapter calling to witness the natural world
and human history. The heaven full of constellations referred to here is
also the human heart which receives spiritual revelation. The trench
refers to an incident in Yemen when a group of believers, probably
Christians, were forced by their persecutors to jump into a burning
trench. They were, however, saved through their faith in God.

95
At-Tín, The Fig

In the name of Allah, the Beneficent, the Merciful.
By the fig and the olive,
and Mount Sinai,
and this secure City,
We have created human beings in the best of forms,
and brought them low,
except for those with faith and good actions,
for their reward will never fail.
Can you dispute the justice of this?
Is God not the wisest of all judges?

The fig and the olive may symbolize Adam and Abraham, respectively, who with Moses are among the fruits of God's Garden. The City is Mecca.

106
Al-Quraish, The Quraish

In the name of Allah, the Beneficent, the Merciful.
For the covenant of security with the Quraish,
allowing caravans in Winter and Summer,
let them serve the Lord of this House,
who provides food for their hunger,
and security from fear.

The Quraish are a powerful tribe of Mecca to which Muhammed belonged and which he united and made strong in faith.
As one places one's faith in God, one finds protection through the covenant made with mankind in pre-eternity.

101
Al-Qári'ah, The Day of Astonishment

In the name of Allah, the Beneficent, the Merciful.
By the Day of Astonishment,
what is the Day of Astonishment?
What will make you realize
that something is going to stun you?
One day mankind will be like scattered moths,
the mountains like fluffed wool.
Then, whoever has goodness in the balance
will have a tranquil life.
But whoever's balance is light
will have the abyss for a home.
How can We tell you what this would be?
A fiercely blazing fire!

The title of this chapter is sometimes translated as "The Calamity,"
which, unfortunately, conveys only the negative aspect of that final
moment when each soul shall be "stunned or astonished" at the summa-
tion of its life on earth. This day may have a personal and a universal
meaning. The day when mankind will be like "scattered moths" could also
describe the present time. The word for scattered, "mabthuth," is the
word in contemporary Arabic for the broadcast of radio waves. The
fiercely blazing fire of the last line may be that emotional inferno that is
the consequence of continued evil actions and negativity.